The Majesty of Natchez

REID SMITH
JOHN OWENS

PADDLE WHEEL PUBLICATIONS
Post Office Box 386
Prattville, Alabama 36067

D'EVEREUX

1840

When William St. John Elliott built *D'Evereux* in 1840, he placed a rare jewel in the abundant crown of ante-bellum Natchez. So elegant is *D'Evereux,* so perfect are its proportions, it is almost as if some ancient Greek builder were the sole architect of such beauty. Even its name, borrowed by Mr. Elliott from his mother's maiden days, has a pure and poetic ring.

The site St. John Elliott chose for his home was an 80 acre tract, lying alongside the Old Trace. Here, in the midst of a grove of gently swaying live oaks, he built *D'Evereux.* From Europe Mr. Elliott imported his own landscape artist to terrace and till the soft luxurious soil of his gardens. All about *D'Evereux* there was an Eden of rarest camellias, spreading blankets of multi-colored azaleas, wandering banks of sweetly scented roses. For a time life at *D'Evereux* was disturbed only by the gliding swans who chased their shadows across the limpid glaze of the lake in the rear gardens. These were the bountiful days when St. John Elliott's good friend, Henry Clay, came to *D'Evereux* for a visit and stayed long enough to have his portrait painted by the French artist, Bahin. The grand ball given here in Clay's honor is said to have been one of the most elaborate functions in Mississippi's history. On this night *D'Evereux* glowed with the light of more than 3000 candles.

Legend has it that on one of Clay's frequent visits to *D'Evereux* he was so disheveled from his arduous trip that one of Mr. Elliott's slaves mistook him for an unwelcome vagabond and set the family dogs on the distinguished Senator from Kentucky. Luckily, Mr. Clay was recognized before any real damage was done.

Mr. Elliott, who died in 1855, was spared the sight of seeing Union troops destroy his beautiful gardens when they camped at *D'Evereux* during the War. Just before their coming, Mrs. Elliott had the family silver buried on the grounds. Fate would have it that the Federal commander pitched his tent on the very spot where the treasure lay hidden. Fortunately, however, the silver was never discovered.

It was also during the soldiers' stay at *D'Evereux* that the two murderers of George Washington Sargent of *Gloucester* were hanged on its grounds.

Long years later, after the clouds of war had rolled away, *D'Evereux* became the center of a more pleasant drama, when a well-known movie company filmed "The Heart of Maryland" beneath its great oaks.

Although St. John Elliott's limpid lake has evaporated like the years, and its swans have chased their shadows into eternity, *D'Evereux* today has been restored to its rightful role as one of the real showplaces of ante-bellum Natchez.

© 1969, by

PADDLE WHEEL PUBLICATIONS

All rights reserved. No parts of this book may be reproduced in
any form without permission in writing of the publisher.

ISBN 0-911116-67-2
Library of Congress Catalog Card #72-97471

To

DICK and MAVIS FELTUS,

*through whose friendship
and many kindnesses we came
to know and love, not only
the old homes of this city,
but the people who live in them;*

and to

*the founder and guiding spirit
of the annual Natchez Pilgrimage,*

MRS. J. BALFOUR MILLER,

*a great southern lady who has done
so much to preserve the remnants of
a truly colorful era in man's march
through time.*

Acknowledgments

We wish to express our deepest gratitude and appreciation to all of the fine people of Natchez who, with their special brand of warmth and hospitality, have contributed so much to the compiling of this book. Although space permits listing of property owners only, we want to acknowledge the many courtesies extended to us by the numerous hosts, hostesses, and caretakers, who gave so generously of their time to make our task easier. Particular thanks go out to Miss Zelma Pylant of Natchez, the young lady who so graciously and patiently posed for the picture in the opening section of this book. And, finally, to the following home-owners, to whom "The Majesty of Natchez" owes an everlasting debt:

The Ayres P. Merrill Family of *Airlie*

Mrs. Anne Gwin Vaughn of *Arlington*

The City of Natchez for *Auburn & Choctaw*

Dr. & Mrs. Robert H. Barnes of *The Barnes Home*

Dr. Harold C. Hawkins & Mr. H. Hal Garner of *Brandon Hall*

Mr. & Mrs. Charles Kelley of *The Briars*

Mr. & Mrs. Barnett Serio of *The Burn*

The Natchez-Adams County Chamber of Commerce for *The Chamber of Commerce*

Mr. & Mrs. Charles J. Byrne of *Cherokee*

Mrs. Douglas H. MacNeil of *Cherry Grove & Elms Court*

The Natchez Garden Club for *Connelly's Tavern*

Mr. & Mrs. William Carl McGehee of *Cottage Gardens*

The Natchez Historical Society for *The Coyle House*

Mr. & Mrs. T. B. Buckles of *D'Evereux*

Mr. & Mrs. T. B. Buckles, Jr. of *D'Evereux*

Mr. & Mrs. Tom L. Ketchings of *Dixie*

Mr. & Mrs. N. L. Carpenter of *Dunleith*

Mr. & Mrs. Richard Campbell of *Edgewood*

The W. S. R. Beane Family of *Elgin*

Mrs. A. K. Ellis of *Ellislee*

Mrs. Joseph B. Kellogg of *The Elms*

Mrs. Walter P. Abbott of *Elward*

The National Society of Colonial Dames for *Evansview*

Mr. & Mrs. Bazile R. Lanneau of *Fair Oaks*

The Morrison Family of *Gloucester*

The Beltzhoover Family of *Green Leaves*

Mr. & Mrs. Harold Leisure of *The Griffith-McComas Home*

Mr. & Mrs. Hyde D. Jenkins of *Hawthorne*
Mr. & Mrs. Earl Hart Miller of *Holly Hedges*
Mr. & Mrs. J. Balfour Miller of *Hope Farm*
The State of Mississippi for *Jefferson Military College*
Mrs. Jeanne Modesitt of *King's Tavern*
Mr. & Mrs. George M. Marshall of *Lansdowne*
Mr. & Mrs. Singleton Gardner of *Lansdowne*
Mrs. Frank Fauntleroy of *Linden*
Mr. & Mrs. Kelly E. McAdams of *Longwood*
Mrs. George M. D. Kelly of *Melrose*
Mr. S. H. Lambdin of *Mistletoe*
The Heirs of Mrs. Hubert F. Barnum of *Monmouth*
Mrs. Hunter Goodrich & The Kendall Heirs of *Monteigne*
The National Park Service for *Mount Locust*
Mr. & Mrs. Ferd Sessions of *Mount Repose*
Mr. & Mrs. McVey Butler of *Myrtle Terrace*
Mr. & Mrs. Lawrence Adams of *Oakland*
Mr. & Mrs. Orrick Metcalfe of *The Parsonage*
The Presbyterian Church for *The Presbyterian Manse*
Mrs. Louise Metcalfe Williams of *Ravenna*
Mrs. Roane Fleming Byrnes of *Ravennaside*
The John Shelby Marshall Family of *Richmond*
Mr. John F. Banks of *Riverview*
The Mississippi Society Daughters of the American Revolution for *Rosalie*
Mrs. Laurie G. Ratcliffe of *Routhland*
Mr. Charles E. Ratcliffe of *Routhland*
Mrs. Edward R. Howard of *Routhland*
Mrs. Davidson R. Smith of *Saragossa*
Mr. & Mrs. Walter Scott of *The Scott Home*
Mr. & Mrs. John Smith of *The John Smith House*
The Williams Estate for *Springfield*
The Pilgrimage Garden Club for *Stanton Hall*
Dr. & Mrs. George W. Moss of *Texada*
Mrs. Doris Green of *The Towers*
Dr. & Mrs. Homer A. Whittington of *Twin Oaks*
Mr. John B. Lombardo of *Villa Lombardo*
Mr. & Mrs. L. A. White of *Wigwam*

Welcome
to
NATCHEZ

Come, take a trip with us across the threshold of time.
Leave behind the cares of this moment to stand refreshed again
in the long shadows of the great White-Pillared Past that
quietly lingers here. Thread your way among the lines of history
that have been written high on these Bluffs. Bend your ear
to the whispered intrigues of the wily Aaron Burr, who so often
passed this way. Plant your feet along the paths down which
Andrew Jackson marched toward battle or strode in timid
courtship. Listen for the lilting laughter and melodious notes
of gay soirees led by the great Lafayette. Stand witness in
the fog of an early morning duel on Vidalia Sandbar as
more than one proud gentleman, in search of honor,
shakes the hand of Death instead. Stop too, for an instant
to peer into the wayward ramblings of the mighty Mississippi,
upon whose brawny, brown shoulders all the glories of
ante-bellum Natchez, somehow, always came to rest.
Once your foot falls upon this doorstep, your own
hometown may never seem the same.

Under Five Flags

It seems that the Bluffs of Natchez have always drawn men to their heights. Climbing 200 feet above the rampaging whims of the mighty Mississippi, these cliffs have long held out to Man a haven of safety and a promise of plenty.

The Natchez Indians had chased the buffalo and worshipped their sun gods here for generations before the first Whites ever wandered this way. Before they would surrender their hunting grounds, the crown of these cliffs would swim in a sea of blood.

The first European to covet the potential of the Bluffs was LaSalle. Drifting downstream in search of the Mississippi's mouth this great explorer, as early as 1682, recognized that whoever controlled these heights could well control the river. Several years later Bienville, agreeing that the flag of France would do well to fly from these crests, raised Fort Rosalie here in 1716.

For more than a decade the soldiers of Louis XV and the sun-worshipping Natchez shared the Bluffs in peace. Tragedy struck swiftly though, in 1729, when the French commander, deciding to take a certain sacred Indian village for his own, caused The Natchez to swoop down upon the royal garrison and massacre it almost to a man. Although the French soon returned to take their vengeance on the Indians, the days of France on the Bluffs were even now in their twilight.

In 1764, at the close of the French and Indian War, the Union Jack of Britain was flung to the breeze above Fort Rosalie. The Crown began making huge land grants to encourage settlement. By the time of the American Revolution enough Englishmen had tasted success here to remain loyal to the King. When trouble came, it was brought by the Spanish.

Once she was sure George III had his hands full of rebellion on the Eastern Seaboard, Spain moved in for a quiet take-over of Natchez. Deciding on a role of gentle dominion over their newest province, the Spanish outstripped the British in their bestowal of free land. A new prosperity emerged and, while Natchez held fast to the Anglo-Saxon customs of the snuff-sniffing Englishman, its architectural landscape began to take on a definite Latin flavor here and there.

With the Revolution over, the Americans who had fought it were free to venture south and westward. By 1798 the elegant Dons of Natchez were to taste the hard-fisted truth that they must abandon the Bluffs forever.

A treaty in 1801 with the remaining Indian tribes opened the Natchez Trace to wagon travel and mail deliveries and started a landslide of settlement by the Americans. Ten years later the first steamboat docked at the wharves Under-the-Hill and ushered in "King Cotton's" fabulous reign of nearly 50 years of undreamed of abundance. By 1830 only New York City could count more millionaires than Natchez.

Even during the Civil War fate still smiled on Natchez. Though occupied early by the Federals, except for a few random shells from a Union gunboat, the city felt little of the pain of battle.

With Appomattox, Natchez again looked to the River and "the good earth" for its salvation. Fate though, had turned her face away. That new-fangled monster, the railroad, gradually swept the great steamboats from the Mississippi and stranded Natchez in a world of weed-choked cotton fields and ruptured family fortunes.

When better days came to the rest of the country, these "good times" by-passed Natchez. Instead of tearing down old landmarks to make way for progress and the craze for late Victorian gingerbread, Natchez could only afford to patch up here, dab a little paint there, and cling to the white-pillared beauty of a more abundant past.

In 1932 this ironic quirk of fate was seized upon by a little group of courageous ladies, who sought to share the special heritage of their town with the rest of the world. Out of this desire to introduce others to "The Majesty of Natchez" arose the now far-famed annual Pilgrimage, a bright new epoch in the story of a city that UNDER FIVE FLAGS of change has, in reality, changed so little.

THE CONFEDERATE PAGEANT

Since 1932 and the beginning of the annual Natchez Pilgrimage *The Confederate Pageant* has reigned supreme as the highlight in a month-long series of festive events.

Staged and produced in its entirety by the members of the Natchez social swirl, *The Pageant,* through tableaux and dance, turns back the hands of time. Amid the roll of distant drums the flags of five great nations march from the pages of the past, each saluting the end of one era and the beginning of another in the long and colorful role call of Natchez' history. Here too, once again, if ever so briefly, "King Cotton" returns to his throne, a man's home is his castle and his lady again a queen.

STANTON HALL
1851

In creating a suitable "ornament for the town" where he gained his great wealth, Frederick Stanton bequeathed to Natchez a landmark in time, magnificent *Stanton Hall*.

Begun in 1851 and christened first *Belfast* in honor of Frederick Stanton's Irish origins, it was to take six years to build this house.

Determined to seek the best materials and craftsmanship money could buy, work was hardly underway when Mr. Stanton sent his contractor and architect, Mr. Thomas Rose, off to Europe to see first hand to their selection. Arriving overseas, Mr. Rose selected English silversmiths to create the Sterling doorknobs and massive Sheffield hinges. Out of Italy came the ornately carved Carrara mantels and rose-patterned iron for the balconies. The great gold leaf mirrors for the 70-foot combination front parlor and music room were French, as were the uniquely handsome bronze chandeliers to be swung throughout the house. To haul all of this finery to the Bluffs of Natchez, Frederick Stanton had Mr. Rose charter an entire sailing ship, spent the then outlandish sum of $83,262.23 to build *Belfast* and died in less than three months after moving into his new home.

The rain of the Lower Mississippi Country had hardly smoothed Frederick Stanton's grave, when the Civil War ushered in a period of tragic ordeals for his beloved *Belfast*. First, a shell from a Union gunboat blasted away a portion of one of the great Corinthian pillars. Next, as if to add insult to injury, blue-clad troopers were billeted for a time in *Belfast's* servants' quarters.

Reconstruction had brought new hardships and the 1890's found *Belfast* a fashionable school for young girls and the name changed to *Stanton Hall*. Later years were no kinder. On one occasion the First Bank of Natchez put this old mansion on the block for a price less than the cost of its iron fence. In 1940 though, a new light shone on *Stanton Hall's* future when the house and grounds were bought by The Pilgrimage Garden Club as a restoration project. Alas, again a suitable "ornament for the town," *Stanton Hall*, with its delightful Carriage House Restaurant next door, today serves as headquarters for the world famous annual Natchez Pilgrimage that has been held since 1932.

CONNELLY'S TAVERN
Circa 1795

From high on the crown of Ellicott's Hill, *Connelly's Tavern* looks back on time to those days when Spanish grandees strutted the Esplanade, and scare-crowed pioneers stumbled along the Old Trace that wandered beneath the graceful, sunlit galleries.

Built first as a residence, half brick, half frame, and in part from old ship timbers, *Connelly's Tavern* first began its career as an inn and ale-house under the early hand of old Pat Connelly and his wife. This was just before the surveyor friend of George Washington, Andrew Ellicott, used the tavern's heights to raise the first American flag ever to fly over Natchez. The next year, 1798, Isaac Guion led a shaggy troop of Revolutionary veterans into town to back Ellicott's contention that Natchez was on the United States side of the 31st parallel and that the Spanish Dons must go. Capt. Guion's threats worked. Overnight, on March 29, 1798, the Spaniards gave up the city to the Americans.

Pat Connelly and his wife were still the proprietors when the Duke of Orleans, later King Louis Phillippe of France, packeted downriver, stayed for a time at the hilltop hostelry, and probably had his royal dignity shocked by some of the tavern's rules: "No more than five to sleep in one bed." "No Boots to be worn in bed." "Organ Grinders to sleep in the Wash house," etc.

Connelly's Tavern was destined to have other famous customers besides the Duke. At another time Aaron Burr and Harmon Blennerhasset huddled in the old taproom to plan their defense in their upcoming treason hearing.

Connelly's Tavern would likely have been lost to the ages had it not been for The Natchez Garden Club which bought it in 1935 and has brought about its completely authentic restoration as the club's headquarters.

STANTON HALL

Upstairs and down, rare antiques provide an encore to the elegance of STANTON HALL.

Frederick Stanton spared no expense in "building an ornament for the town." All mirrors and chandeliers are French. The heavily carved mantels are of the finest Italian marble.

The massive pier mirrors of the parlor and music room are the largest in all of Natchez.

CONNELLY'S TAVERN

Pioneer kitchen recalls days of few hot meals along Old Trace.

In the wild and wooliest era of the Old Southwest, the drawbridges of the Tavern's dry moat were raised at night so second-story sleepers could close both eyes.

The taproom had a special magnetism for great and small alike. Here Aaron Burr dreamed of empire, later planned defense when charged with treason.

PRIEST HOME
Circa 1783

The *Priest Home* has been a part of the panorama of early Natchez since that long ago time when the Red and Gold standard of Spain flew above these Bluffs.

Though originally located on nearby Market Street, this old place in more recent years was moved next door to *Connelly's Tavern* as a restoration project of The Natchez Garden Club. The same is true of the immediately adjoining little building that was *Judge Winchester's Law Office.* The Judge, above and beyond the call of his judicial duties, also had the distinction of overseeing the education of Varina Howell, the second bride of Confederate President Jefferson Davis.

During the days of the Dons in Natchez, the *Priest Home* was the residence of a much beloved Catholic padre, Father Lennan. While the earliest records are somewhat sketchy, it is believed that Father Lennan made his home here for at least 15 years prior to the American take over of the city in 1798. The moment, however, the good Father realized the Spanish were gone for good and that the new masters of Natchez were here to stay he immediately sold his house on Market Street.

The date on Father Lennan's bill of sale, March 27, 1798, makes the *Priest Home* the first house in Natchez to change hands under the new American regime. Only the night before, the Spanish at Fort Rosalie had cased their colors and to the doleful shuffle of muted drums marched away into the dark night of history.

SCOTT HOME
1796

Snuggled demurely against the sidewalk on North Pearl Street, just beyond the long reaching shadows of mighty *Stanton Hall,* is the *Scott Home.*

This seemingly tiny cottage once cost Mississippi's first printer, Andrew Marchalk, but five hundred dollars. Like so many well-to-do fathers of his day, Marchalk felt called upon to furnish a home for each of his daughters as they married. The *Scott Home* was a wedding present to his youngest daughter, Jane Elenore.

MYRTLE TERRACE

Early 1830's

The most exciting chapter in the story of *Myrtle Terrace* was written in the swirling currents of the mighty Mississippi by a blue-eyed, bushy-faced, oath-slinging giant of a steamboat man, Capt. Tom Leathers of the *Natchez*.

Stocking-footed, Cap'n Tom stood six feet four and "dressed out" at a booming 270 pounds. A legend in his own time, Tom Leathers was not the kind to turn down a challenge for a race, not even when it came from wily, hard-driving John Cannon, Master of the steam packet *Robert E. Lee*. New Orleans to St. Louis was the distance. The purse would be $20,000—winner take all. Not since Fort Sumter had such a fever of excitement swept the land. Word of the race even overflowed into the betting parlors of London and Paris. When it was all over, fortunes large and small would touch new hands on both sides of the Atlantic.

From the beginning, as both boats swung upstream from New Orleans in the twilight of June 30, 1870, it was a question of Capt. Cannon's cunning against Capt. Leathers' confidence. The *Lee* had been stripped to the waterline of any and everything that would hamper its speed, even to the paintings on the cabin walls. The *Natchez*, on the other hand, steamed away from the dock with a full cargo and a long passenger list. Before it was over barrels of pitch and lard had been gulped by the boilers of both boats, the *Robert E. Lee* had stuck for a time on a sandbar below Cairo, and Capt. Leathers had hesitated six hours in a fog bank to protect his passengers and kiss "good-bye" the $20,000 purse.

Such was the man who bought *Myrtle Terrace* in 1854 and lived here in peace for eight tranquil years. He died on a New Orleans street beneath the fragile wheel of an unknown bicylist, who peddled fast away from the great hulk of a man who had never run from anything.

JOHN SMITH HOUSE
Circa 1825

Though built well after the beginning of the American era, this quaintly demure story-and-a-half cottage has about it a certain Spanish flavor. Always kept to perfection, the *John Smith House* is one of the truly distinctive "little gems" of Natchez.

ELLISLEE
Circa 1800

Located originally on a winding country lane the Aaron Killingsworth Ellis home, *Ellislee,* today finds itself tucked away in the heart of Natchez. Even so, the long and leisurely yawn of this old home's slimly-columned galleries lends to the corner of State and Pine a subtle voice of the Indies. Here, if but for a moment, may be heard the soft lapping of a gentle surf, the faint whisper of a timid tropic breeze.

Aside from the loosely woven beauty of its facade one of *Ellislee's* proudest possessions is a handsome rosewood bedroom suite that once belonged to Jane Green, the daughter of Col. Thomas Marston Green. It was Col. Green who married his friend, Andrew Jackson, to Rachel Robards at *Springfield* plantation in 1791.

To the rear of *Ellislee* is found one of the few detached old brick kitchens in Natchez that is still in use.

CHAMBER OF COMMERCE
Circa 1820

Like a piece of Old World charm in miniature, the home of the Natchez-Adams County Chamber of Commerce is but a hop, skip, and a jump from two of the city's main tourist attractions—*Stanton Hall* and *Connelly's Tavern.*

16

KING'S TAVERN

Before 1789

Most will concede that historic *King's Tavern* is the oldest house in Natchez—perhaps in all of Mississippi. Certain deeds prove beyond all doubts that this ancient hostelry was here when what little there was of Natchez was still Under-the-Hill.

Resembling a pre-Revolutionary War blockhouse, *King's Tavern* must have been a welcome sight to the weary wayfarers of the Old Trace. From far and wide they came: flatboatmen from the Ohio; backwoodsmen from Olde Kaintuck and Tennessee; besatined dandies from the East; out of the Devil's Punch Bowl, barefooted river pirates; and from parts unknown, lean, hungry, highwaymen, quick to offer a pocket of swag for a bowl of broth. Reeking with the smell of hard ale and rumbling with the coarse voices of even harder men, *King's Tavern* was a haven and melting pot for all.

Stacked together from a conglomoration of cypress planking, sun-cured brick, and massive ship's timbers, the *King's Tavern* of pioneer days had to be of sternest stuff. Even now there can be found in the main doorway the scattered bullet holes left by an early Indian attack.

The old brick steps leading from the sidewalk up to the *Tavern* have been gouged thin by the shuffling footfalls of time. Could they but speak they might well recall that memorable day long ago, when the first U. S. Mail to reach Natchez was brought here over the Old Trace by an Indian runner.

VILLA LOMBARDO

Late 1800's

With 13 rooms above and 13 rooms below, it is obvious that the builder of *Villa Lombardo* was not a superstitious man.

Situated near the foot of Jefferson St., right at the point where the Old Trace swung south along the River, *Villa Lombardo* has served many roles in the long and colorful life of "The City on the Bluffs." Although its actual construction date is obscure, the numerous peepholes in its many interior doors gives more than a little credence to owner John B. Lombardo's contention that *Villa Lombardo* had its origin as a house of ill-repute.

In later times *Villa Lombardo* was to have a more respectable station, first as a residence and later as *Ellicott Inn*, a quaintly charming restaurant operated by the ladies of The Natchez Garden Club and bearing the name of Maj. Andrew Ellicott, the gritty American patriot who raised the first U. S. flag just across the way at *Connelly's Tavern.*

Since 1957, when this old place came under the ownership of Mr. Lombardo, it's doors have been open to antique collectors from the world over. Here at *Villa Lombardo* is found, not only fine glassware, handsome copper, and rare period furnishings, but also the easy-going hospitality that is so much a part of the Natchez tradition.

The fine selection of antiques housed at VILLA LOMBARDO is enough to whet the appetite of the most avid collector.

VILLA LOMBARDO'S ancient iron gateway has become a trademark of Natchez hospitality.

THE BURN
Circa 1835

The story of *The Burn* is highlighted by many odd twists of fate.

Had 21-year-old John P. Walworth not left his Cleveland, Ohio home one day long ago the interesting saga of *The Burn* may never have had a beginning. Traveling by steamboat on his way to New Orleans in quest of his fortune, chance had it that John Walworth took a brief shore leave in Natchez. So much did he like what he saw that he stayed on, immediately prospered, and eventually built *The Burn*. A few years later Mr. Walworth's very dear friend, Gen. William T. Martin, the builder of *Monteigne* was to end up in Natchez in the very same manner.

The Burn owes its unusual name to a small stream that once meandered near the outer-bounds of John Walworth's tremendous estate. It is of Scotch derivation, meaning "The Brook." Built originally as a two-story house, *The Burn,* shortly after its completion, oddly enough, did burn. The top floor was gutted by fire, and the roof line was changed to what it is today.

Another quirk of fate connected with *The Burn* had its beginning during the Civil War just before the siege of Vicksburg when the Union gunboat *Essex* appeared below the Natchez bluffs. At the time Maj. Douglas Walworth, at home at *The Burn* on sick leave, was urged to lead a local guard unit, the Silver Grays, in the defense of the city. Hasty shots were fired. A bombardment of Natchez followed, killing little Rosalie Beekman, the town's only casualty and an aunt of a latter day owner of *The Burn*, Mayor S. B. Laub.

During the Union occupation, what was one of the first houses selected as a headquarters and hospital? *The Burn*, of course.

CHOCTAW

Circa 1835

When it comes to architecture, Natchez has it all. For instance, there is a flavor of Charleston about the huge mass of brick and stone that is *Choctaw*. The way the great white columns seem to rise right out of the street, with its double entrance from the sidewalk, *Choctaw* may just as well be down on the Battery as in the heart of Natchez.

Built originally by Joseph Neibert as a town house, *Choctaw*, with its appropriate Indian "cross-sticks of war" baluster decorations, was deeded away in 1845 as the "first free school in Natchez." Befittingly, too, *Choctaw*, now owned by the American Legion, is right across the way from another Indian namesake, *Cherokee*.

CHEROKEE
1794-1810

Always resplendent in the sunlight of afternoon *Cherokee* owes its lofty perch to an old Spanish superstition.

When Jesse Greenfield began planning his Natchez home in the early 1790's, he came face-to-face with a strict Spanish ordinance which forbade any sort of excavations within the city. It seems that "His Most Catholic Majesty's" provincial officials were firmly convinced that the dreaded scourge of that day—Yellow Fever—lurked below the ground. As a consequence Jesse Greenfield chose the crown of a hill for the main body of his house. By letting the rear portion follow the natural contour of the landscape he could gain an extra story for the back of his home. When wealthy David Michie added the white-columned Classic front in 1810, *Cherokee* became one of the most imposing split-level homes in ante-bellum Natchez.

For a time the Michies lived the typically abundant life in their town house on the hill. These were the days of primly pruned terraces, and the soft rustle of scurrying servants. These were the nights of swishing satins as silk-stockinged gentlemen waltzed their ladies 'til the dawn.' This was the world David Michie left behind when he died suddenly in 1820—ironically enough, it is thought, from Yellow Fever.

Following the depression years of the 1830's the title to *Cherokee* passed to the great land baron, Frederick Stanton. It was while residing here that Mr. Stanton began to dream of his noble Irish beginnings and conceived the idea of building the palatial mansion that was to become *Stanton Hall*.

Today, with its gleaming white facade, elaborate interior, and picturesque rear gardens, it is hard to imagine that *Cherokee* once changed hands for the paltry sum of eight thousand dollars.

Spring sunshine and gay blossoms
have a way of joining hands each
year to paint a blazing panorama
of beauty across the rear gardens
of CHEROKEE.

The entrance hall of WIGWAM
bids a hearty welcome to one
of Natchez' most uniquely
charming old houses.

WIGWAM

Before 1790

The unusual charm of *Wigwam* today is a fitting tribute to the labor of love that so recently reclaimed it from the oblivion of the ages. 'Twas but a short while ago when *Wigwam*, one of the oldest homes in the city, echoed to the ring of hammer and nail and felt the warm glow of fresh paint for the first time in generations—thanks to two youthful Natchezians, Dr. Harold C. Hawkins and Mr. H. Hal Garner.

Timbers uncovered in the central portion during the restoration date this section of *Wigwam* before 1790. Other additions, such as the four spacious upstairs rooms and center dormer window, came with a renovation done in 1839. Other than repairs and restoration few changes have been made in *Wigwam* since that date. The ceilings and walls of the old ballroom are even today still decorated with the gala flourishes of the famous French Empire painter, Dominique Conova.

The delicate iron lacework framing the recessed front entrance is some of the most beautiful to be found north of New Orleans' French Quarter. The alternately arched doorways of the interior are also especially interesting.

Wigwam is believed to have derived its unique name from having been built originally atop an Indian burial mound. Many trinkets and ancient relics are continually being unearthed on its immediate grounds.

This grand old place, presently owned by Mr. and Mrs. Buzz Harper, houses some of the finest antique furniture and china to be found in all of Natchez.

THE TOWERS
Circa 1818-1854-1927

This beautiful old home occupies a prominent niche in the jigsaw puzzle of antebellum Natchez architecture. Better than any other in town, *The Towers* typifies the warmth and charm of Adriatic Italy. The Renaissance itself somehow loiters for a moment in the deep shadows of the triple-arched entrance while time seems to walk with guarded footsteps across a yard of giant azaleas.

Elegant and poised against a framework of magnolias, *The Towers* stands today unscarred by the 1927 blaze that swept away its third-story chambers at each end of the house. But here too, legend is mindful of that tragic day in the 1860's when a Federal officer quartered in *The Towers* sent out the order to burn Frank Surget's majestic town house, *Clifton*—all because Mr. Surget had neglected to include him on the guest list of a grand ball.

COTTAGE GARDEN
1793-1794

Basking in the warm southern sun, amid spacious lawns, *Cottage Garden* looks back to the Spanish days of Natchez for the heritage of its beginnings.

As resplendent and sturdy as ever after a recent restoration by the William C. McGehees, *Cottage Garden* once stood at the hub of a huge royal land grant to one Don Jose Vidal. Being of noble birth and an officer of the local Spanish garrison, it is not surprising that young Vidal's estate should reach all the way to the River and the infamous Devil's Punch Bowl and include a portion of what is now the National Cemetery, not to mention all of the site of Charity Hospital.

The Vidal tenure at *Cottage Garden* was, however, to be of brief duration. With the 1798 cession of the Natchez Country to the United States Capt. Vidal found himself transferred

across the river to Post Concordia. About this time tragedy again struck at the youthful officer with the death of his beloved wife. Legend has it that she was buried on the high Natchez bluffs so that, from across the river, he could view her grave.

In more modern times *Cottage Garden* itself has taken on a somewhat nautical flavor. It seems that during the recent restoration numerous rope holes were found in many of the old timbers, indicating that some old sailing ship out of the remote past may have been gutted to furnish materials for the gallant Don's New World home.

AIRLIE

Before 1790

At one end of Myrtle Avenue is a shadowy sanctuary of ancient cedars. Here is *Airlie*.

Once owned by such illustrious Spanish grandees as Don Jose Vidal and Don Estaban Minor, this quaintly rambling old place may well be termed "The Charm Cottage of Natchez". Low of ceiling and hugged together by peg and tongue-and-groove, *Airlie* is one of the oldest houses in this city of antiquity.

When the Federals came to town during the Civil War *Airlie* was chosen as a Union hospital and there are no few stories today about the bloodstains that once besprinkled its hand-hewn floors.

At war's end *Airlie* came under the hand of Aylette Buckner and, since the descendants of this family have lived here ever after, this old house is a treasure chest of priceless heirlooms. Fine oils of the greats of yesteryear hang from low Spanish walls, and rare sets of Old English and Rose DuBarry china spread themselves across a world of antique mahogany and hand-carved rosewood.

Such furnishings are a real part of AIRLIE'S special charm.

RIVERVIEW

Circa 1840-1869

Riverview has lingered long in shade-drenched places. Although the records of the building of the oldest portion of this house are rather vague, it is definite that a structure stood on this spot prior to 1841. This section was incorporated into the main body of *Riverview* which was erected by an ex-lieutenant in the Confederate Army, George M. Brown, about 1869.

With the terrible tornado of 1841 still vivid in his memory, Mr. Brown built brick walls 13 inches thick with all interior partitions anchored to the foundation. And, as if this were not reassurance enough, he had a large cellar dug out beneath his home.

The site upon which *Riverview* now stands once belonged to John Steele, a veteran of the Continental Army and onetime acting governor of the Mississippi Territory. Before Steele, the property was a part of the extensive holdings of the colorful Spanish grandee, Don Jose Vidal. Still another official of "His Most Catholic Majesty", Don Estaban Minor, once held the title to the grounds of present day *Riverview*. Additional historical flavor is added by the fact that during the Civil War one of the boundaries of the Union's Fort McPherson ran through this property.

As impressive as *Riverview's* lineage of ownership may be, it is the informal beauty of the grounds and the rare antique treasures of the interior that give to this old place a particular niche in the vast array of ante-bellum Natchez homes.

The sumptuous dining hall of D'EVEREUX has hosted many an early American notable. One of the most frequent of the famous guests to take a repast of mutton and Madeira here was the great Henry Clay of Kentucky.

EDGEWOOD

Early 1850's

Jane Bisland Lambdin was a gentle lady of simple tastes. Since this was a rare virtue in the golden days of the Old South Samuel Lambdin was especially determined to please his wife. Their home might have its white pillars but they must be humble in their proportions and have a real purpose in their stance. There could be more than one story, but there must be no pretense toward enormity. Out of his desire to yield to truth yet retain a subtle flair of his lavish age Sam Lambdin gave his house a guarded and unique demeanor that has always been the special charm of *Edgewood*.

If Samuel and Jane Lambdin's home was denied the imposing countenance of some of its more pretentious contemporaries, *Edgewood* could boast certain conveniences they did not share. One of these was a dumb waiter that delivered the family's meals, steaming hot, from the basement level slave kitchen to the main floor dining hall. *Edgewood* also sported an inside storage tank from which water was piped to several of its upper rooms. Only Natchez' majestic *Montebello* and the regal *Windsor,* near Port Gibson, could lay claim to such luxuries.

Gazing serenely across a gently folding lawn of oak and evergreen, *Edgewood* stands on ground once included in an ancient Spanish land grant to Jane Lambdin's grandfather, John Bisland. Located in the historic Pine Ridge section of Natchez, this fine old place lies between two other well-known homes in this area—*Mount Repose* and *Mistletoe,* both of which were also once part of the great Bisland estate.

Though many distinguished notables visited here in those early days, one of *Edgewood's* most frequent guests was James Reid Lambdin, a much acclaimed portrait painter of his time and a brother of Samuel Lambdin. In the pleasant natural peacefulness that has always been a hallmark of *Edgewood,* James Lambdin is said to have created some of his finest works.

The grounds of EDGEWOOD.

LANSDOWNE
1853

When Charlotte Hunt married George Marshall, the newlyweds received a 600 acre wedding present from the bride's father, "King David" Hunt, one of the wealthiest men in all of ante-bellum Mississippi.

Lansdowne was planned and built by the young couple in the plentiful year of 1853. An artful mingling of Georgian and Greek Revival, the exterior, almost modest at first glance, is somehow deceptive about what lies behind its white facade. From the 65-foot hallway to the spacious bedrooms and yawning ceilings, everything about the interior of Lansdowne is shockingly tremendous!

If this old home had its origin in an era of peace and plenty, the Civil War soon brought violence and havoc to its doorstep. Vicksburg had just fallen when a band of renegade Union looters paid Lansdowne a most unwelcomed visit. Confronted by one of the troopers for her house keys, Charlotte Marshall refused and took a beating about her face, the marks from which she carried to her grave. Although most of the family valuables were saved by a Negro servant who had buried them beneath the front portico, the maurauders, out of sheer spite, left a trail of Lansdowne's fine apricot china behind them all the way to Pine Ridge Road.

Appropriately, Lansdowne, the first home in the state with its own gas light plant, has remained through the years in the hands of the Marshall family.

In LANSDOWNE'S drawing room, original full-length draperies guard against the summer heat, while the first hand-blocked French Auber wallpaper still clings tenaciously to the walls.

LANSDOWNE'S cock-fighting chair is a stark reminder of the days when men had time to sit and watch rather than eat and run.

One of the many nostalgic mysteries of the Natchez Country is the 'Sunken Road'. Such tree-shaded byways were carved out of the landscape by the timeless tread of wagon and carriage wheels over the soft, powdery topsoil known as Loess. This fine dust was blown in from the Middle West centuries ago. It was formed during the Ice Age by the slow grinding of glacier against rock.

MISTLETOE

1807

If Natchez is a portrait of the past, with a flourish of grandeur here and a stroke of drama there, here also can be found the tender touch of the ordinary events of life. Such is the special role of *Mistletoe*.

Styled as "Mississippi Planter" in design, *Mistletoe* was built by John Bisland as a honeymoon cottage for his 19-year-old son Peter and Peter's young bride, demure Barbara Foster of *Foster's Mound* plantation.

Though endowed with a fine education in his father's native Scotland and backed by an impressive family fortune, Peter Bisland soon let it be known that he much preferred the dreams of scholars to the realities of the business world. As others basked in the white-pillared glories of their achievements Peter spent the brief sands of his time pondering the simple beauties of life at *Mistletoe*. Here he concerned himself with climbing roses rather than the mounting price of cotton. While friends opened and closed the doors of banks with their successes and failures Peter Bisland was content to link himself with a world yet unborn. *Mistletoe,* to Peter Bisland, was never meant to be a symbol of how high a man can rise, but more, to him, it ever remained the honeymoon cottage of his own blissful youth.

Since *Mistletoe* has always remained in the Bisland and Lambdin families this little place has a legacy of antique heirlooms that would be the pride of the most pretentious mansion. At *Mistletoe*, though, all are blended perfectly together to breathe a breath of elegance into the humble bosom of a house that has always been a home.

Regal family portraits watch quietly over the cozy warmth of MISTLETOE'S cypress paneled sitting room.

This Nobleman's Chair dates to the days of Merrie Olde England.

The huge Ming vase in MOUNT REPOSE'S living room is surrounded by countless heirlooms that have been in the Bisland family for generations.

MOUNT REPOSE
Before 1824

One glimpse of *Mount Repose* is enough to tell how this old plantation home got its name. Crowning a gentle slope in the Pine Ridge section of Natchez, *Mount Repose,* with its airy galleries and easy grace is part and parcel of its peaceful realm of gray-bearded oaks and faintly sighing southern breezes.

Mount Repose was built before 1824 by William Bisland, son of John Bisland, a shrewd old Scotch planter who began his fortune with a 552 acre Spanish land grant in 1782. Constructed alongside what was then the King's Highway, *Mount Repose* has never left the ownership of the Bisland family. Scotsman that he was, old John Bisland, were he here today, might well be especially proud of this.

William, perhaps as firm of purpose as his father before him, was not a man to back away from his word. A staunch disciple of the great Henry Clay, he once made the statement that the proposed drive to the front entrance of *Mount Repose* would never be opened until Clay became President. Since Clay was never elected the drive was never opened during William Bisland's lifetime—nor has it been since. The approach to the house is still toward a side wing.

Because *Mount Repose's* ownership has been as untampered with as William Bisland's word, it is today the homestead of family heir-looms aplenty. One of the most interesting pieces to be found here is a slave-made cherry desk that belonged to Judge W. B. Shields. The Judge, then Col. Shields, had the unique distinction of assisting in the 1807 arrest of Aaron Burr only to be the ex-Vice-President's chief defense counsel when Burr was up for indictment a short time later.

EVANSVIEW
Circa 1790-1830-1860

By 1860 swarthy Josef Bontura had pocketed enough gold from his Under-the-Hill enterprises to climb The Bluff. A Portugese by birth and a wine merchant by trade, Bontura brought to the narrow, two-and-a-half-storied house he bought near the mouth of Silver Street not only a new prosperity, but the Latin's traditional love for outdoor balconies and cast iron frills. Whether Josef Bontura actually added the definite Creole touches, or whether they were already present and just caught his fancy, no one can be sure. Though certain old maps and drawings of the Spanish Esplanade and Parade Grounds indicate that the rear portion of Bontura's house was here before 1790, the exact date of its beginnings and additions is as vague as the precise moment of a sunset. The arched secondary wing that gives the home its L-shape and helps form the quaint side courtyard seems surely to have

Scarlett O'Hara's bed in "Gone with the Wind."

been the handiwork of Bontura since the ground level served as a combination carriage house and stable. The new owner from Under-the-Hill was known far and wide as a lover supreme of fine horseflesh and handsome coaches.

Another innovation that definitely came from the ex-wine merchant was a change of names for the old home—from *The Market House* to *Bontura*—and so it remained until far later days when it came under the ownership of Mr. and Mrs. Hugh H. Evans and was eventually donated to the National Society of Colonial Dames of America in the State of Mississippi. Around this time *Bontura* was renamed *Evansview*.

(Continued on next page)

The noble arches of EVANSVIEW'S carriage wing recall the days when Josef Bontura prided himself as owning some of the finest blooded horses ever to prance the Bluffs of Natchez.

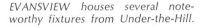

EVANSVIEW houses several noteworthy fixtures from Under-the-Hill.

Mrs. Evans was a co-author of the romantic history, "They Found It In Natchez" and of "A Day In Natchez."

Evansview has known many colorful hours. In its huge banquet hall have been entertained such notables of their day as Stephen Foster, Capt. Tom Leathers of the steamboat Natchez, and Mark Twain. From the balcony of Evansview a multitude of Natchez' most elegant looked on breathlessly as Capt. Leathers made his famous riverboat race with the Robert E. Lee. In less gay days Evansview had one of its brick walls damaged by a shell from the Union gunboat Essex. Housed, however, in the front upstairs bedroom is a far more pleasant reminder of Civil War days, the handsome four-poster bed used by Scarlett O'Hara in the filming of "Gone With The Wind." The bedspread was crocheted especially for the picture by Mrs. Audley Stammreich, well-known Natchezian of nearby Richmond.

Peter Little spared no expense when he built THE PARSONAGE to satisfy the yearnings of his devout Eliza. Even the rear of this ministerial manor house is a thing of beauty.

THE PARSONAGE
1840

If Peter Little was a man of strong will and great wealth *The Parsonage* is proof positive that he also had a patient and generous heart.

Most of Peter Little's early days had gone toward carving a fortune from his lumber business and making the climb from Under-the-Hill to the top of The Bluff. By 1820 he had arrived, and for his young wife Eliza he had built *Rosalie* as a great white-pillared symbol of his success. For Peter Little this handsome Georgian mansion was to become a temple of the pleasures of his day and means. Peter's devout Eliza, a childhood convert of the pioneer evangelist, Lorenzo Dow, let it be known however that such was not to be. Rather than a host to gay soirees and carefree evenings, Eliza insisted instead that *Rosalie* serve as a halfway house for every circuit-riding preacher who ventured into Natchez with Hell-fire in his saddlebags and Damnation on his tongue.

Suddenly one day in 1840 the idea struck Peter to build *The Parsonage*. Such a place, located just across the way, would provide a haven for Eliza's itinerant minister friends and Peter's own home could alas become his castle.

After being deeded outright to the Methodist Church by the Littles in 1853, *The Parsonage* was later sold as a private home. There followed a string of owners for more than a quarter century. Fortunately though, in 1893 this old place came into the hands of Mrs. James M. Metcalfe and has been the home of her descendants ever since.

ROSALIE
1820

When the Yellow Fever of 1806 struck down the Jacob Lowes, Peter Little promised to look after their freckled-faced Eliza. Not knowing what else to do he married her in her 13th year and, on their wedding day, sent her off to school in the East. After her return a few years later as a copper-haired, green-eyed beauty, he built her an exquisite Georgian mansion—*Rosalie*.

Here, on the historic site of the old French fort, lumberman Little envisioned the staging of grand balls and lavish levees befitting his hard-won station in the Natchez social swirl. But Eliza, a childhood convert of the great evangelist, Lorenzo Dow, had different ideas. In no time Peter Little's *Rosalie* became a rest stop for circuit-riding Methodist preachers. Finally, out of agreeable desperation, Peter offered to provide Eliza's minister friends a separate haven and *The Parsonage* was built nearby in 1840.

Sixteen years later both Peter and Eliza Little were dead without an heir and in 1857 the Andrew Wilsons moved into *Rosalie*.

When New Orleans fell early in the Civil War and Union gunboats plowed upriver toward Vicksburg the Wilsons wrapped their handsome parlor mirrors in blankets, buried them in the ruins of old Fort Rosalie and stepped quietly aside as U. S. General Walter Gresham, a kind and courtly invader, moved his wife and staff into *Rosalie*. Though the General finally had to banish Mrs. Wilson to Atlanta as an underground Confederate agent, the Greshams and the Wilsons became such friends that when the war was over General and Mrs. Gresham came back to *Rosalie* for a visit.

Now owned by the Mississippi Society of the Daughters of the American Revolution *Rosalie* still bears on its wide-planked floors the scars of Union spurs, some of which may even belong to General U. S. Grant, since he spent three days here during the occupation.

Child's bed and doll furniture date to ante-bellum days.

This canopied four-poster was the bed used by General U. S. Grant during a visit to Union headquarters at ROSALIE. On display in the entrance hall downstairs is a sofa on which the General took his afternoon naps.

The double parlors at ROSALIE have to be the most elegantly furnished rooms in the house. The complete set of Belter rosewood furniture, in the parlors since 1858, is one of the few in existence. The great gold-leaf mirrors were buried in a hillside, when the house was occupied by the Federals in 1863.

DIXIE

1795-1828

Built in 1828 as a town house by Samuel Davis, *Dixie* today represents one of the city's most complete and courageous restorations of recent years. Only a short while ago, before Mr. and Mrs. Tom L. Ketchings came upon the scene, *Dixie* was hardly more than a dim reflection of its past glories. Mr. and Mrs. Ketchings gave two laborious years toward completion of the seemingly impossible task of restoring what was once a decaying shell to the classic town house it was always meant to be.

The oldest portion of *Dixie*, the rear dependency, probably came at the hand of one Maurice Stackpoole as early as 1795. Just prior to this time Stackpoole had received the property under a Spanish grant requiring him to erect a residence here within one year or return the land to the Crown. It remained though, for Samuel Davis to build the fine red brick house with the graceful Doric columns.

Since the first master of *Dixie* was an older brother of Jefferson Davis, it is likely that the future Confederate President was a frequent visitor in this home. At a later day the younger Davis would return to woo and win for his second wife, the beautiful

Varina Howell of *The Briars*. During the civil War *Dixie* was owned by still another illustrious family—the Bowies, kinsmen of the great frontier knife fighter, Jim Bowie, who died at the Alamo. Fate would have it that the flashing blade that carved out Bowie's special niche in history was, like *Dixie*, also designed and built in Natchez

Next door to DIXIE, Mr. and Mrs. Ketchings operate a most interesting antique shop.

COYLE HOUSE

1793

The *Coyle House* stands on a land grant from Don Gayosa, one of Spain's first governors, to Hugh Coyle, one of Natchez' first tailors.

With its sturdy severity, the *Coyle House* is strikingly similar to St. Augustine's "Oldest House in the United States." Fortunately, it was saved from oblivion in 1960 when the Natchez Historical Society undertook its restoration.

TEXADA

1792

But for the efforts of Dr. and Mrs. George W. Moss, the old Spanish Quarter of Natchez may have lost to the ages one of its most enchanting buildings.

Once the residence of Don Manuel Texada, this old place has served many roles—from home to tavern house and even as a meeting place of the Territorial Legislature.

When completely restored by Dr. and Mrs. Moss, *Texada* will regain its rightful place as one of the city's most historic buildings.

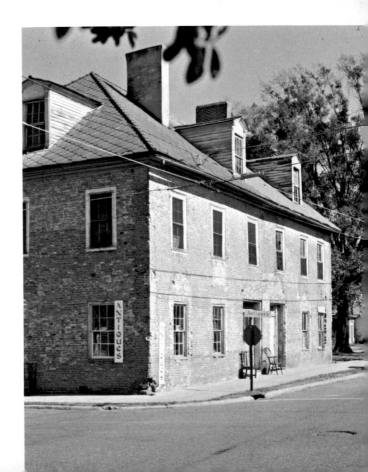

GRIFFITH-McCOMAS HOME
Circa 1794

The *Griffith-McComas Home,* along with *Connelly's Tavern,* may well be the finest example of West Indian architecture in the whole of Mississippi. Too, the long swing of its hospitable galleries are somehow strangely synonymous with the surname of its present owners, Harold and Bonnie Kate Leisure.

Probably built by Leonard Pomet, the *Griffith-McComas Home* has been the property of many distinguished families. Counted among its past masters is the Rev. Daniel Smith, who organized Natchez' First Presbyterian Church in 1817, and the founders of Mississippi's State Bar Association, the Messrs. John and William Griffith. Anna Willis Mc-Comas, a relative of George Washington, once resided here following the death of her husband, Gen. Josiah Hillen McComas. The General, a onetime Mayor of Natchez and commander of the troop that welcomed Lafayette to the city in 1825, was a close friend of Andrew Jackson and had served under "Old Hickory" at the Battle of New Orleans.

The Leisures, who came to Natchez from the "Crescent City" some years ago, have completely restored this fine old place and now operate a quaint little bookshop here.

The little bookshop in the GRIFFITH-McCOMAS HOME has on display many rare and contemporary editions. Numerous publications dealing with the lore of the Old South may be found on its shelves.

HOLLY HEDGES
1796

When Don Juan Scott received his Spanish land grant where *Holly Hedges* now stands, his deed, dated 1795 and signed by Gov. Gayoso, contained a right unusual restriction. There were to be no bullfights in the side yard under any circumstances. Undaunted by this strange decree Don Juan Scott built his new house the following year in the heart of Old Spanish Natchez.

From the Don's heirs, *Holly Hedges* passed to Judge Edward Turner. In time, the Judge was to make the house a wedding present to daughter Mary when in 1832 she became the bride of John T. McMurran, a law partner and brother-in-law of Gen. John Quitman. The new owners, smitten with the Greek Revival fever of their time, added many of the Classic touches so prominent in *Holly Hedges* today.

The McMurrans remained in their home on the southwest corner of Washington and Wall until their upswinging fortunes enabled them to build *Melrose,* a more imposing reflection of their new station.

After the McMurrans, *Holly Hedges* had a considerable list of separate owners. One was Fanny Bontura, widow of old Josef Bontura, the Portugese wine merchant who had once made a fortune in Natchez Under-the-Hill.

Fortunately for *Holly Hedges,* this old house in 1948 came into the hands of two master restorationists, Mr. and Mrs. Earl Hart Miller. Under their artistic eye and talented touch the house has been reworked from the depths of its Spanish-tiled cellar to the eaves of its twin-dormered roof line. *Holly Hedges'* simple outer beauty belies the regal antique splendors so tastefully housed within.

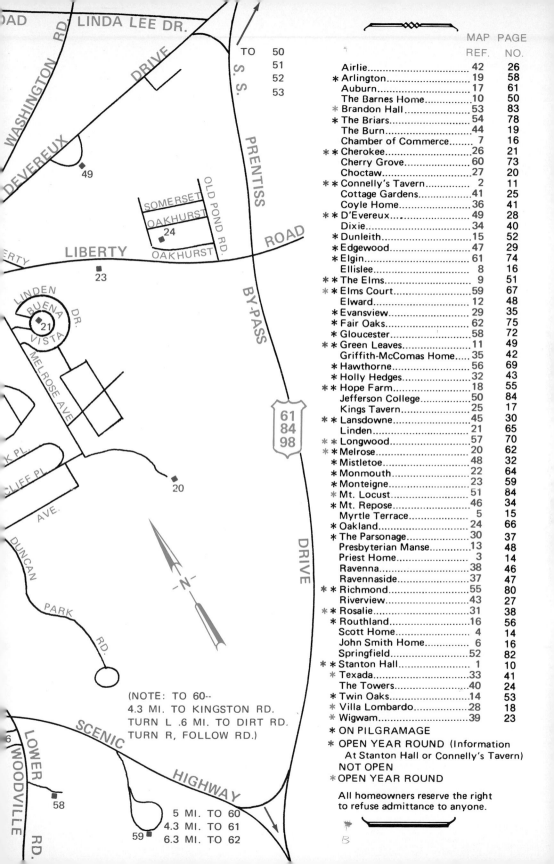

ROAD
LINDA LEE DR.
WASHINGTON RD.
DRIVE
DEVEREUX
S. S.
PRENTISS
49

SOMERSET
OAKHURST
OLD POND RD.
24
OAKHURST
LIBERTY
ROAD
ERTY
23

BY-PASS

LINDEN DR.
BUENA VISTA
21
MELROSE AVE.

K PL.
CLIFF PL.
20
AVE.

DUNCAN
PARK RD.

-N-

DRIVE

(NOTE: TO 60--
4.3 MI. TO KINGSTON RD.
TURN L .6 MI. TO DIRT RD.
TURN R, FOLLOW RD.)

LOWER WOODVILLE RD.
SCENIC
HIGHWAY
58
59

5 MI. TO 60
4.3 MI. TO 61
6.3 MI. TO 62

TO 50
51
52
53

61
84
98

* ON PILGRAMAGE

* OPEN YEAR ROUND (Information
   At Stanton Hall or Connelly's Tavern)
   NOT OPEN

* OPEN YEAR ROUND

All homeowners reserve the right
to refuse admittance to anyone.

B

RAVENNA

Circa 1835

Some of the stories that have through the years attached themselves to *Ravenna* are almost as colorful as the springtime that splashes a blaze of glory across this wisteria world of wild honeysuckle and softly sighing willows.

One such story has to do with courageous Zueleika Metcalfe, an early mistress of *Ravenna,* who used the nearby bayou to smuggle food to hungry Confederates during the Federal occupation of Natchez. With three sons serving in the southern ranks, it was no secret how Oren and Zuleika Metcalfe felt about the Union invaders. For their strong sentiments, and because of Mrs. Metcalfe's food deliveries along the bayou, the family was banished from *Ravenna* for the duration of the war. With the end of hostilities, however, the Metcalfes returned to their beloved home—but without one of their three sons. Tom never came back from Gettysburg.

In the hallway at *Ravenna* is a portrait of Dr. William Rousseau Cox. William was the son of Dr. John Coates Cox, a most adventuresome kinsman of the Metcalfes. Around John Coates Cox centers one of the most unusual coincidences in American history. When Dr. John Cox was a young man he once went in quest of Africa's fabled city of Timbuktu. While on this venture the doctor was saved from death by a native African tribesman, "The Prince of Jallon," a son of the Emperor of Timbuktu. Some years later, as chance would have it, Dr. John Cox was startled one day to find his old friend, "The Prince," now a slave, peddling sweet potatoes on the streets of Natchez. From that moment on Dr. Cox spent the rest of his life trying to gain freedom for "The Prince." At the doctor's death, his son, William, took up the cause and never gave up until "His Highness" and his whole family were once again safely home in the land of Timbuktu.

RAVENNA'S entrance hall,
with its stairway framed in
a gracefully vaulted arch, is
one of the most beautiful
in Natchez.

RAVENNASIDE, standing near
the entrance to the grounds
of RAVENNA, is the home of
Mrs. Roane Fleming Byrnes,
a descendant of Oren and
Zuleika Metcalfe. It has been
largely through the efforts of
this charming southern lady that
the recently begun
restoration of the Old Natchez
Trace was undertaken.

47

ELWARD
Circa 1842

More than one architect of note has dubbed *Elward* "The Little Gem of Natchez" because of its purity of design and flawless detail.

Built about 1842 by Richard Elward, this little house was selected by the Historic Building Survey, as "possessing exceptional historic or architectural interest and as being worthy of most careful preservation . . ."

THE PRESBYTERIAN MANSE
Circa 1820

When Benjamin Wade came to the Natchez Country at the end of the 18th Century, he brought with him a comfortable stake of $25,000. Almost overnight, through his cotton factoring and planting interests, Wade turned this into a fortune.

The home he built next door to *Green Leaves* is proof enough, however, that Mr. Wade had a yearning for beauty as well as wealth. Nearly perfect in its modest proportions, this mansion-in-miniature has one of the most beautiful entrances in all of Natchez.

Purchased by the Presbyterian Church in 1838 for $16,000, this charming little place has remained *The Presbyterian Manse* ever since.

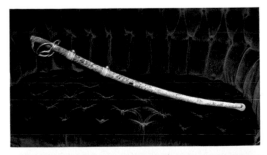

One of the most treasured heirlooms at GREEN LEAVES is the bullet-scarred saber that once belonged to Col. Daniel Beltzhoover. A relic of the Battle of Waterloo this handsome weapon was a present from a young Englishman who served under the Colonel at Vicksburg.

This pistol once swung at the side of Natchez' most famous fighting man, General John Quitman. It was a personal gift from the General's granddaughter, Alice Lovell, to Melchoir Roch Beltzhoover. Both the gun and the case bearing Quitman's name are on display today in the front parlor of GREEN LEAVES.

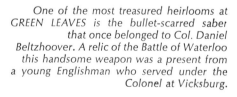

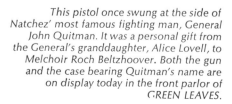

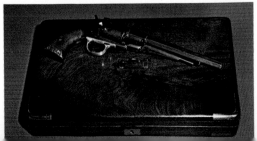

GREEN LEAVES
Before 1812

The original portion of *Green Leaves* was here before the War of 1812. It was built by Jonathan Thompson who, as it turned out, had little chance to enjoy his new town house. Thompson, his wife and their three children were all destined to die within a single week during the Yellow Fever epidemic of 1820.

In 1849 *Green Leaves* was to pass to George Washington Koontz, the man who had come down out of Pennsylvania as a youth, worked his way to a partnership in Britton & Koontz Bank, and became such a trusted friend of Jefferson Davis that the Civil War found him in Europe negotiating loans for the Confederacy.

Mr. Koontz not only added to *Green Leaves* and made it what it is today but was also the founder of the family that still resides here. It was his daughter Virginia who married Mr. Melchoir Beltzhoover and 'twas their son who took as his wife none other than the granddaughter of William Britton, Mr. Koontz' old banking partner.

Out of the merger of these three families, *Green Leaves* has become a museum of antiquity. Among its countless treasures are personal letters to Mr. Koontz from President Davis, a set of china said to have been hand-painted by Audubon, a bullet-scarred saber from the Battle of Waterloo, and a liqueur set from each of the Britton and Koontz families. Not so cherished at *Green Leaves* is a bullet hole in the transom of the main entrance, left there by a would-be assassin of Mr. Koontz during the dark days of Reconstruction.

Indian council oak in rear garden of GREEN LEAVES.

BARNES HOME
Circa 1830

The *Barnes Home* adds a flavor of New England to the varied punch bowl of Natchez architecture. Severe of line and sturdy in stance, it may seem at first glance to have been built by some "ex-Connecticut Yankee" who sauntered South one day over the Old Trace but could not forget the Puritan heritage of his childhood.

Actually there were three homes in early Natchez that were prefabricated in Ohio and shipped by barge down the river. The *Barnes Home* was one of these. The recent restoration of this old place by Dr. and Mrs. Robert H. Barnes revealed, however, that the interior hardware was made locally. Two of the locks in the present-day den were found to bear the label of L. Fitzpatrick, the early Natchez foundryman who forged the first Bowie knife.

Climbing gracefully from the entrance hall to a height of three full stories, the oval stairway of the *Barnes Home* has a swirling delicacy that makes it one of the most beautiful in Natchez.

This iron stairway, once outside, became an important part of the entrance hall when THE ELMS underwent a face-lifting just before the Civil War.

THE ELMS
Circa 1782

Since *The Elms* was a part of Old Natchez before the days of written records it is impossible to pinpoint its exact building date or its builder. Some say it was Don Pedro Piernas of the Royal Spanish Artillery. Others give the credit to William Barland, who received a 105 acre land grant from "His Most Catholic Majesty" in 1782.

Whether Piernas or Barland, there can be little doubt that *The Elms* is a child of the Spanish era. Only Spaniards built ceilings so low, verandas so wide, and walls so thick. The exquisite stairway in the entrance hall also smacks of the taste of Old Spain. Once rising against an outside wall these spiral steps became the focal point of the interior when the south wing was added to *The Elms* in 1856.

Called by authorities " . . . one of the loveliest specimens of Provincial architecture in the state," *The Elms* has had many a colorful owner, from the first High Sheriff of the Mississippi Territory to a straight-laced Presbyterian minister, the Rev. George Potts.

As unique as its owners is *The Elms* itself. One especially interesting oddity was a call bell system that ran from a pull cord in each room back to the old rear gallery. Since each bell differed in pitch, the house servants knew exactly which room was calling.

By way of a water supply there were three old brick cisterns in the outside gardens. Winter rains were piped in from the roof to these underground reservoirs. The cistern in the front garden was for drinking only, while the two in the rear were used for laundry and cooking.

The Elms, in the same family now for four generations, has long been regarded one of the true gems of Old Natchez.

DUNLEITH
1847

Majestic! This is the word for *Dunleith*. Like a mighty Grecian temple this great manor house rules the oak-shaded lawns that fold gently away on every side. Once it took such a home as this to satisfy a kinsman of kings.

But if *Dunleith's* builder and first lord, Charles Dahlgren, was a direct descendant of Sweden's King Gustavus Adolphus and the son of that country's first U. S. consul he had an even more important asset, he was the duel-fighting, quick-tempered, second husband of old Job Routh's daughter, Mary. In those days Mr. Routh was a man of mountainous means and generous habits. As each of his children married it was his custom to parcel out a portion of the 1700 acre Spanish land grant from which he had carved a fortune. To Charles and Mary, Job Routh gave the site of his own home—the first *Routhland,* demolished by a lightning fire in 1845. It was on this very spot that the Dahlgrens built *Dunleith.*

Conceived in an Old World taste for classic elegance and born of the New World's ability to pay for it, *Dunleith* provided Natchez with one of its most imposing reminders of the days when cotton was "King."

'Twas only fitting that Joseph Carpenter, beloved philanthropist and "Cotton King" in his own right, should one day become master of *Dunleith.* Since that time five generations of the Carpenter family have enjoyed the majestic splendor of an old home that seems never to have heard the passing footfall of the years.

TWIN OAKS
1812

Twin Oaks was built in 1812 by Jonathan Thompson, a dealer in early Natchez real estate who gave the city its first subdivision.

The house, originally called *White Cottage,* was constructed on a parcel of land set aside in an old family estate for the "building of a residence for the Second Son." The "First Son" had received a similar plot across the way and had named his home *One Oak.* In honor of this early "Second Son" and in deference to a deed "which spoke of the Two Large Oaks in the front," the present owners, Dr. and Mrs. Homer A. Whittington in more recent years appropriately changed the name to *Twin Oaks.*

Among the earliest residents of *Twin Oaks* was the Rev. Pierce Connelly and his wife, Cornelia. During Rev. Connelly's tenure as Rector of Natchez' Trinity Episcopal Church two of their children were born at *Twin Oaks.* After a time, however, both Pierce and Cornelia Connelly decided to embrace the Catholic faith. Arriving in Rome, their children were placed in the care of the Vatican Orphanage. Pierce went into the priesthood and Cornelia entered a nunnery. Eventually sent to England to found a new Catholic order, Mother Connelly is presently in the process of beatification and probably someday will become St. Cornelia. The quaint little chapel in the rear gardens of *Twin Oaks* was built in her memory.

While *Twin Oaks* has had a lengthy list of masters, it remained for the Whittingtons to retrieve this old house from the despair of neglect. It was during their extensive restoration that an accidentally spilled drop of acid revealed that all of the door hardware in *Twin Oaks* is of the finest Sheffield silver!

Today the tastefully landscaped grounds of roses, tulips, and evergreens, combine with an elegantly furnished interior of Boulle, Belter, and a host of rare French antiques to make *Twin Oaks* one of the true showplaces of ante-bellum Natchez.

The dining room at TWIN OAKS is French Victorian, while the china is from the famous Italian house of Ginori. Another one of the "Little-Big" houses of Natchez, TWIN OAKS is a literal treasure chest of fine antiques.

HOPE FARM's living room houses a handsome six-octave piano above which hangs a portrait of Mrs. J. Balfour Miller, founder of the annual Natchez Pilgrimage.

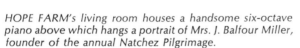

HOPE FARM'S ancient kitchen houses wooden Indian figurehead from steamboat Natchez. Ingeniously designed Punishing Chair was used by early schoolmasters to get across a point of discipline.

HOPE FARM
1775-1789

Hope Farm, as quaintly charming as its name, traces its lineage back to the days when the Union Jack of Britain floated over Natchez.

Truly one of the city's finest "Little-Big" houses, *Hope Farm* was built in two parts. The first, or rear wing, was constructed by one Marcus Hoiler in 1775. The front portion was added in 1789 by a new owner, the great Don Carlos de Grand Pre, a Spanish governor of the territory. This accounts for the distinctly low overhanging eaves and stuccoed wall of the deep front gallery. Each reflects the Latin's traditional love of outdoor leisure. Perhaps, too, this is why the Don left intact the early rear wing with its double-decked veranda opening onto one of the real charm spots of *Hope Farm,* the rear garden.

When the J. Balfour Millers came to *Hope Farm* in 1927 they brought with them a special love of antiquity. They would repair and restore, but never tamper with the special charm of their new home.

Since both Mr. and Mrs. Miller could trace their heritage back to Colonial days many of the furnishings they moved into *Hope Farm* were priceless family heirlooms. In the years that followed, many other fine pieces were added so that today more than one authority has called the interior of *Hope Farm* ". . . a connoisseur's delight." Within this house are furnishings representative of every period of Natchez' history. In addition, *Hope Farm* probably has the best equipped pioneer kitchen in the city.

Even more important to Natchez, however, is the fact that Mrs. J. Balfour Miller had the early foresight and lasting energy to found and promote the annual Pilgrimage that has been enjoyed since 1932 by thousands of visitors from over the world.

ROUTHLAND

Circa 1817

It is next to impossible to point to the exact building date of *Routhland*. Certain records, however, indicate that this fine old home stands on ground once granted to Job Routh by the Baron Carondelet in 1792. Thirty-two years later Job deeded to his son John "ten acres and a dwelling" that was very likely the beginning of the present day *Routhland*.

If Job Routh was somewhat of a Croesus of his time, son John had his own successes and is known to have shipped as many as 4000 bales of cotton to European mills in a single season.

After a time, the Routh family was to have its share of ups-and-downs. Caught in the Panic of '37, there was nothing left but to sacrifice *Routhland* to the auction block. There followed a series of brief owners until the house and grounds were purchased in 1871 by ex-Confederate General Charles Clark. General Clark, who had also served as a wartime Governor of Mississippi, brought an unusual kind of fame with him to *Routhland*. He once had the unique distinction of reading his own obituary. The notice had been published by a Vicksburg newspaper friend who had prematurely given the General up for dead from wounds received in the fighting around Baton Rouge.

Other masters of *Routhland* were to follow General Clark but it remained for its present owners, the Ratcliffes, to restore this fine old home to its past glory and give new meaning to the words of an early visitor from New England: "There can be no ostentation in a people who hide their dwellings from the public road."

The beautiful parlor at ROUTHLAND lends a special flavor to a house that, in every other way, is geared for informal life.

Imported chandelier in ROUTHLAND'S dining room very rare and distinctive.

"Gold Drawing Room" at ARLINGTON represents the epitomy of luxurious living in the Old South's "Age of Abundance."

ARLINGTON
1816

Though an ominous legend still clings about the death of its widowed young first mistress, it is the sheer beauty of *Arlington* that quickens the pulse of nostalgia.

In separating fact from fantasy, this we do know of *Arlington*—this stately old place, begun in 1816 by Jane Surget White, was four years in the building and has been acclaimed one of the finest white-pillared mansions of its kind to be found anywhere.

That Jane White could afford the very best of everything is understandable since she was a daughter of Pierre Surget, the great land baron. 'Twas only natural, too, that Jane White should have a demanding taste for fine architecture. Her own late husband, Capt. James Hampton White, but a short while before had been engaged to come South from New Jersey to design the first bank building in Mississippi.

If *Arlington* and its English-landscaped grounds have their own special beauty, the exquisite Georgian doorway of the main entrance offers new wonders inside. Here, beneath *Arlington's* 17-foot ceilings, is the famous "Gold Drawing Room," an 8000-volume library of the rarest editions, original oils by Vernet, Sully, and Audubon, a 1000-member family of early dolls and an antique glass collection that has few peers anywhere.

MONTEIGNE

1855

Had young William Martin not stopped off in 1842 for a visit with an old friend, Natchez would have had no *Monteigne*.

Chance would have it, though, that William T. Martin, did linger in Natchez long enough to become a schoolmaster while still 21, a district attorney at 22, the bridegroom of *Linden's* Margaret Dunlop Conner in 1854, the builder of *Monteigne* the following year, a Confederate Major General during the Civil War, and the father of 13 children along the way.

Of French Huguenot stock, 'twas but natural that General Martin chose a chalet design for his mansion. So too it was that he gave his home the Old World family name—*Monteigne*.

For the General's wartime service with "Jeb" Stuart in Virginia and Joe Wheeler in Tennessee, his beloved *Monteigne* paid a tragic price. During the Union occupation of Natchez, cavalry horses were ridden through the magnificent entrance hall and French drawing room, imported crystal chandeliers stripped from their moorings, and General Martin's private papers "flung to the four winds."

Today the scars of those bitter days have been erased and *Monteigne* dwells ever-so-peacefully in a floral wonderland of heavily banked azaleas and softly climbing wisteria. Here and there more than 350 rare varieties of camellias push open their blooms to smile back at the warm southern sun.

Floor of MONTEIGNE'S entrance hall once bore scars from hoofs of Union cavalry horses.

Collection of rare camellias at MONTEIGNE numbers into hundreds.

AUBURN'S free-standing spiral stairway is marvel in design and grace.

AUBURN
1812

Some say *Auburn* was the first of the great white-pillared mansions in Natchez. Others argue that *Gloucester* got its classic facade before *Auburn* was finished. All agree, however, that architect Levi Weeks built for Lyman Harding a most imposing home.

In 1815, at the death of Mr. Harding, *Auburn was* bought by Dr. Stephen Duncan, an erstwhile Pennsylvanian come South to make his fortune. And make his fortune Dr. Duncan did—so much so that he soon became one of the first millionaires in the United States.

Always moving in the most prominent circles, Dr. Duncan was the attending physician that day over on Vidalia Sandbar when merchant prince Abijah Hunt was killed in a duel with George Poindexter, Governor and later U. S. Senator from Mississippi. Among the many notables to visit the Doctor at *Auburn* were Henry Clay, Edward Everett Hale, and the composer of *Home Sweet Home,* John Howard Payne. Even these great personages must have been favorably impressed by the hand-carved woodwork of the entrance and banquet halls, drawing room, smoking and "family dining rooms." Surely great and near-great alike were awed by the beautiful free-standing stairway that spirals, unsupported to *Auburn's* second floor.

Once the owner of more than 500 slaves, Dr. Duncan in later years paradoxically became an avid Abolitionist. So strong was his stand on the slavery issue that when the Civil War came he left Natchez to spend his last days up North. In 1911 Dr. Duncan's heirs deeded *Auburn* and its grounds to the City of Natchez with the stipulation that the recreational facilities to be built here could be used free of charge. So vast were *Auburn's* grounds that they now embrace several tennis courts, a swimming pool, dance pavilion and a 210 acre golf course.

MELROSE'S green and gold tête-à-tête became the ante-bellum version of the modern game table—once the center cushion was removed.

MELROSE'S bateau, with its cushioned center arm, served as a built-in chaperon for young lovers of the ante-bellum age.

MELROSE
1845

When the John T. McMurrans built *Melrose* in 1845, obviously the "Age of Abundance" had become a way of life in Natchez. No pillar could rise too high, nor the cost of raising it be too great. If the "proof is in the pudding," *Melrose* must rank as the very essence of Old South elegance.

Having married double first cousins, John McMurran and John Quitman of nearby *Monmouth* were not only kinsmen, but very prosperous law partners. For two decades this prosperity was reflected in the luxurious lives of the McMurrans of *Melrose*. Little did anyone realize that John McMurran, like General Quitman, was somehow a scion of the tree of tragedy. As poison ended the General's days in '59, not only did the Civil War sweep away the fortunes of John McMurran but a steamboat fire was to take his life the year following Appomattox.

The second master of *Melrose*, Mr. George Malin Davis, himself a prominent attorney, was the forebear of a new dynasty and one that has held ownership from 1865 to the present. As a consequence, the magnificent furnishings and appointments housed inside *Melrose*, the breathtaking gold and green and rose brocades of the double parlors and the great solid mahogany punkah of the dining hall have remained virtually untouched by the finger of time. Here too, is found a landscape of early Natchez, the only one ever painted by John James Audubon.

To the rear of *Melrose* are the outbuildings. In a state of perfect preservation even today they still house the servants' quarters, the mansion's own dairy and the old kitchen, in use as such even now.

The rear of MELROSE, almost as beautiful as its front, was a bustling courtyard of activity in bygone days.

An original landscape of early Natchez
by Audubon is found in the dining
hall at MELROSE.

A handsome Early Victorian étagère holds many priceless family heirloms.

MONMOUTH
Circa 1818

There is about *Monmouth* the rock-ribbed strength of its most famous owner, Gen. John A. Quitman.

Built around 1818 by the John Hankinsons, *Monmouth,* with its massive square columns and broad-shouldered façade is in every sense a man's house. *Monmouth,* too, through the decades has been a temple of triumph and tragedy.

The Hankinsons had been in their mansion on the hill but a short while when an act of kindness suddenly ended their happy lives together. Befriending one day, a stranger stricken with Yellow Fever, John Hankinson and the stranger were both dead of the disease within the week.

A short time after Mr. Hankinson's death, *Monmouth* was to pass to the hand of its most illustrious tenant.

John Quitman's rise to fame and fortune was as dynamic as was his personality. One moment he was a relatively unknown First Captain of the blue-coated Fencibles that escorted Lafayette ashore on his 1825 visit to Natchez. Next, we find him at Judge Edward Turner's ball where the Grand March was led by the famous Frenchman and the Judge's beautiful niece, Eliza. Perhaps it was this very night that John met and charmed Eliza Turner, the future mistress of *Monmouth.* The rest is history: War with Mexico; John Quitman as a Major General, leading the charge on Chapultepec and hoisting the American flag over the Mexican capital; his triumphal return to *Monmouth;* the governorship of Mississippi; election to Congress; and finally his painful death from poisoning at a banquet for President Buchanan in 1859.

Truly, the story of *Monmouth* is found in the life and times of John Quitman.

LINDEN
Circa 1785-1818-1840

Linden is by far one of the oldest of the "Big Houses" of ante-bellum Natchez. Although the actual construction date and the name of the builder are unknown there is reason to believe that the two-storied middle section goes back to 1785.

The sprawling 98-foot gallery and two side wings were added in 1818, when *Linden* came into the hands of the Hon. Thomas B. Reed, one of Mississippi's first United States senators. Credit is also given Sen. Reed for adding the handsome front entrance. Crowned with an exquisite Adam fanlight and flanked with alternating diamond and oval side-panels, this is probably the most photographed doorway in Natchez. More than once it has been featured by Hollywood as a flavorful backdrop in some romantic movie of the Old South.

The rear additions to *Linden*, one of which housed the old kitchen and servants' quarters, came in 1840 when the house was bought by Jane Gustine Conner, widow of Dr. William C. Conner.

If, though, the Widow Conner gave *Linden* its charming back courtyard she was to give far more to her beloved Southland. At the outbreak of the Civil War in '61, this gallant lady sent five sons out from *Linden* to take up arms for the Confederacy. Such sacrifice earned for Mrs. Conner the sobriquet of "Little War Mother," a title she cherished unto her last days.

OAKLAND
Circa 1835

Oakland, as its name implies, is hidden away from the rest of the world in a shade-laced floral fairyland all its own.

In an era when the Greek Revival craze flung great white columns toward the Natchez sky, the builder of *Oakland,* Capt. Horatio Eustis, sought beauty in simplicity. Pure of line, devoid of frill and pretense, this house has all of the characteristics of a typical Southern Plantation Home. There are the exceedingly high ceilings for summer comfort, two huge basement cisterns for a water supply, and a quaint little milk room at ground level. To the rear, and detached from the main house, are the servants' quarters.

Though large and spacious enough inside for the abundance of handsome furnishings so long a part of the *Oakland* heritage, this house was built first of all to be lived in. The solid mahogany doors, possessing as they do a mellow beauty, also afford a subtle reassurance in their silent strength.

If there is a particular room in *Oakland* that calls special attention to itself, it is the library. Here the gracefully vaulted ceiling bespeaks the skilled touch of some unknown shipwright. Throughout the rest of the house the white marble mantels, uncarved though they are, lend a particular warmth and simple dignity to each room.

At a time when great mansions were being built, the *Oakland* of today is proof enough that Horatio Eustis thought first in terms of a home.

ELMS COURT
Circa 1810

Standing today like an exquisite Italian villa at the end of a winding, moss-draped drive, *Elms Court,* for all its present beauty, has had many face-liftings through the years.

Built around 1810 as a simple "double house" of the Federal Period *Elms Court* soon took on the Greek Revival look with the later addition of a white-pillared veranda and a 12-foot deepening of its central hallway. The ironlace grill-work and one-storied wings that give *Elms Court* its special Mediterranean flavor came in the 1850's with the advent of Ayres P. Merrill and his young bride, the former Jane Surget. *Elms Court* was a gift from Jane's father, Frank Surget, one of Natchez' first great millionaires.

For a time life at *Elms Court* was pleasant enough, but for Ayres and Jane Merrill this proved the calm before the storm. Though born to the southern aristocracy of his day, Mr. Merrill, a staunch Unionist at heart, saw the clouds of Civil War snuff out the flames of lifelong friendships and send him North. Here his beloved Jane died without returning to *Elms Court* or seeing her husband appointed Minister to Belgium by President Grant in 1876.

If for the moment *Elms Court* lay wounded by the past, new life flooded in at the hand of another of the great Surgets. This time it was James Surget who again made a wedding present of this fine old place when he transferred title to his daughter, Carlotta, the bride of David Lawrence McKittrick. Suddenly the hearthstones of *Elms Court* glowed with a special warmth. The great hall buzzed now with the frenzied casual chatter of afternoon teas, while into the lean hours of many a morning the light of gay soirees gleamed against the darkness and led one guest of the McKittricks' to call *Elms Court* "The House of a Thousand Candles."

Twin testers at ELMS COURT are real antique rarity.

Victorian bedroom at HAWTHORNE.

The spaciousness of
HAWTHORNE'S interior is
one of the most pleasant
surprises of this fine
old place.

HAWTHORNE

Circa 1814

If Natchez is an ever unfolding city of pleasant surprises, *Hawthorne* must rank near the top of the list. Like *Hope Farm*, this is one of the truly "Little-Big" houses of the Old Trace Country. Modest as a cottage on the outside and spaciously roomy and handsome as a mansion within, *Hawthorne* had its beginnings sometime around 1814—probably at the hand of Jonathan Thompson. Natchez' first great real estate investor.

Whether Jonathan Thompson actually built *Hawthorne* no one can be certain. That he and his wife Anna, a step-daughter of Gov. Winthrop Sargent, once owned it as a summer home is a matter of record. During the Yellow Fever plague of 1825 Thompson and his family were making ready to leave their Natchez town house and seek safety at *Hawthorne* when all fell victim to the disease and died within one week.

Next to follow the Thompsons at *Hawthorne* was George Overtaker, well-to-do proprietor of the famous White House Tavern located nearby at what is now the juncture of Highway 61 and the Lower Woodville Road.

At another time the tragedy of Civil War hit hard at *Hawthorne* when young Robert C. Dunbar, after having just purchased the house for his wife and two small children, marched away to fall in battle.

In recent years *Hawthorne* has come upon far better times and this is reflected in every facet of this fine old home's present day personality—from the perfectly clipped hedges to the intriguing beauty that lies beyond the handsomely fan-lighted double doors of the entrance. Here the watchword is elegance and the password—hospitality, Old South style.

LONGWOOD

Never Finished

Like a page out of "Wuthering Heights," *Longwood* rears its hollow head above primeval woodlands and recalls the tragic days that left it but a monstrous echo of what was meant to be. Conceived as a fabulous reality by wealthy cotton planter, Dr. Haller Nutt, *Longwood*, with the first shot of the Civil War, became an empty, unfinished dream.

Since most of the 70 skilled artisans engaged by Philadelphia architect Samuel Sloan were northerners, there was a frantic dropping of hammers and brushes at *Longwood* the day the news of Fort Sumter arrived. Only the basement floor, where the wine cellar, recreation rooms, and office were to be, had been completed. On the second, third, and fourth floors, half-emptied nail kegs and paint cans were suddenly abandoned to gather the chalky dust of summer evenings. Here and there from a piece of scaffolding the mortar-caked shirt of a slave bricklayer drooped like a headless scarecrow.

Designed as an octagon with four main floors crowned by a fifth-story solarium and sixth floor observatory, *Longwood* was to have had 32 rooms, each with its own outside entrance or balcony. At each level was an eight-sided rotunda. From the first floor, all the way to the glassed-in observatory, was to have spiraled a stairway of Italian marble. Due to the War this majestic stairway never reached Natchez, but the niches to house the classic statuary along its ascent can be seen today.

The 27-inch brick exterior walls of *Longwood*, the countless doorways guarded by recessed panels of solid oak and the great lake-like moat that surrounded this vast domain, are proof enough that Dr. Haller Nutt, like other wealthy southern planters of the '50's, had heard the righteous rantings of the Abolitionists up North and realized they bade no goodwill. For the Nutt family, *Longwood* was to be fortress as well as home. But despite more than $100,000 already spent, another $100,000 and only four months to completion, *Longwood* was doomed to become neither. Here in the basement, the only finished portion of his mansion, Haller Nutt breathed his last on June 15, 1864. Some say he died from pneumonia. Others hold it was from the broken dream that was *Longwood*.

Longwood's temporary dining room in the basement is far simpler than the one Haller Nutt had planned for the upper floor of his mansion house.

Rusting paint buckets and half-emptied nail kegs recall the tragic day when workmen rushed off to war and left LONGWOOD to its hollow destiny.

NATCHEZ-UNDER-THE-HILL

Natchez-Under-The-Hill in the early 1800's could claim the dubious distinction of being the Devil's own personal workshop. Here a burly boatman from the River or dashing dandy from the Bluffs, with the loosening of his purse string, could purchase any or all of the products of Hell wholesale. In this place, during those lusty times along the Mississippi, the only thing cheaper than the body of a woman was the life of a man.

Clinging like a malignant scab to the base of the Bluffs, *Natchez-Under-The-Hill* had no peers as the Sodom and Gomorrah of the Old Southwest. Only four or five muddy streets wide in its hellish hey-day, this city of sin was said to have kept the wheel of chance spinning day and night. More than once the flat rattle of shuffling cards had punctuated the passage of a whole plantation to some dark, river-tanned man with a set of skillful fingers. *Under-The-Hill* whole fortunes, and the people who made and lost them, were known to disappear with the same rapidity.

Today all that remains of *Natchez-Under-The-Hill* is Silver Street and one pitiful row of broken buildings that stare, like hollow-eyed ghosts, across the restless ramblings of the muddy Mississippi.

GLOUCESTER
Circa 1799

The paths of Winthrop Sargent and David Williams had a strange way of crossing. It started the day the stiff-necked, unbending first Territorial Governor of Mississippi took the late Mr. Williams' widow for his second wife. Again their paths crossed when Winthrop Sargent bought the Williams family home, *Bellevue,* doubled the size, hauled four white pillars up to the front, added a second entrance door and changed the name to *Gloucester* for his New England upbringing.

Because Winthrop Sargent could never bring himself to lean with the breeze of his surroundings, he never really became a true piece of the heavy-drinking, lady-loving, duel-fighting jigsaw puzzle of frontier Natchez. Though he was to become wealthy, popularity remained ever beyond his grasp. In part, because of this, *Gloucester,* with its unique dry moat, heavily barred basement windows, and iron-strapped doorways, was as much a vault of safety as it ever was a handsome home for Winthrop and his Maria. Even Gov. Sargent's Last Will and Testament revealed his sense of unpopularity when it requested a simple burial "in the willow yard . . . attended by one-half dozen friends . . ."

A quarter century after the Governor's death the last surviving of his two sons, George Washington Sargent, came back South, bought *Gloucester* off the auction block, and for a time enjoyed a simple life in his childhood home. Then there was that fatal Civil War night when he answered a knock at the door and a marauder's bullet plunged him into oblivion beside his turbulent father who slept so quietly in the little "willow yard" across the way.

CHERRY GROVE
Circa 1788-Rebuilt 1860's

The story of *Cherry Grove* really had its beginning on the teeming wharves of La Rochelle, France, the day Pierre Surget, then a mere sprinkling of a lad, turned his hard, young back on home and stowed away to sea. Crouched in the hold of an 18th Century square-rigger bound for New York, Pierre had little more with him than a strong faith in the future and the rare kind of courage that often walks in the shadow of youth. Combining these valuable virtues with an inborn love of a deck beneath his feet, a few years were to pass before Pierre Surget found himself not only the master of his own ship, but of a new wife as well.

Sprung from hard-working, frugal Huguenot stock, Catharine Hubbard was a perfect mate for a gritty young sea captain with gold in his eye. No more would Pierre sail alone before the mast, for now, alas, his horizons belonged to another.

Together the Surgets bent eager ears to the lush tales of the Lower Mississippi and soon the bow of Pierre's ship was cutting its way through warm southern waters, bound for New Orleans with a cargo of pig iron lying heavy in her hold.

After spending two years in New Orleans, where they lived aboard ship and saw the birth of their first son, Pierre and Catharine finally hauled anchor and steered upstream to Baton Rouge. Here was born another son. Moving on again, further upriver, they at last found their journey's end beneath the great, hulking Bluffs of Natchez. Up there somewhere was a place they would call Home.

Ever a trader at heart, Pierre was quick to strike a deal with a band of local Indians. The cargo of pig iron was bartered for a large parcel of some of the best land in Natchez' Second Creek district. Implemented by an additional 2500 acre Spanish land grant in the same section, Pierre Surget built the family's first *Cherry Grove* here about 1788.

Sometime in the 1860's the original *Cherry Grove* was struck by fire, only to be immediately rebuilt on the same spot where Pierre and Catharine had founded Natchez' Surget dynasty nearly a century before.

ELGIN
1780-1840

Elgin plantation takes up part of an old Spanish land grant to Sir William Dunbar. The grant was made to Sir William as repayment for his services as surveyor of the Province of Natchez.

Peered at through the grove of live oaks that shade its azalea-banked grounds, *Elgin,* at first glimpse, appears as a typical child of the plantation past. A visit behind the 90-foot double gallery, however, reveals the dual personality of this old place. There is the low-ceilinged dining room with its carved oak punkah that dates this portion to the days of Spanish dominion. The more spacious rooms, such as the double parlor separated by handsomely paneled folding doors, were added by Dr. John Carmichael Jenkins in 1840.

Just the year before Dr. Jenkins had taken for his wife Annis Dunbar, the grand-daughter of Sir William, and it was she who named their new home *Elgin,* in honor of her grandfather's old homeplace in Scotland.

During the 15 years Dr. Jenkins lived at *Elgin* the double-decked veranda, a part of the 1840 additions, held few leisure hours for this amazing man. Probably no scholar of his day was so well versed in the field of horticulture as Dr. Jenkins. Almost overnight the grounds surrounding *Elgin* became a living laboratory of grafted orchards and cross-bred fruit trees. Here, too, Dr. Jenkins looked into the possibility of soil depletion and was one of the first to experiment with fertilizers and the shipping of fresh fruit, packed in ice, to far-off northern markets. Perhaps there would have been still more had not the Doctor's life and that of his wife been snuffed out in the Yellow Fever siege of 1855.

FAIR OAKS
Circa 1800

Even though *Fair Oaks* has had three different names and far more owners, there was built into this 98-foot plantation house a special charm that has gone undisturbed for generations.

Jesse Carter was a mere lad, when his family forsook their Virginia origins and in the 1770's wandered southwestward into the Natchez country. Here young Jesse grew to manhood, obtained a major's commission in the local militia, planted his first cotton and married Widow Sarah Canhard of Second Creek.

All records, sketchy though they are, indicate that the spot Jesse Carter chose for his homesite was a 250 acre British land grant to Sarah's first husband. From hand-hewn cypress and old sailing timbers it is believed that the Carters built a long, low, rambling house which they named *Greenoak*. For a time Jesse and Sarah were to share their new home with their daughter, Lydia, and her illustrious husband, George Poindexter, one of the framers of the state's first constitution and later Mississippi's second Governor.

Greenoak's name was changed to *Woodbourn* in 1836 when the house came under the hand of John Hutchins, son of Col. Anthony Hutchins, the first male child of British parentage born in what is now the State of Mississippi. Twenty years later *Woodbourn* finally became *Fair Oaks* with its purchase by Dr. Orrick Metcalfe, a medical graduate of Yale University. Since that time *Fair Oaks* has never left Dr. Metcalfe's family.

The present owners, Bazile and Ann Lanneau, both count their ancestry back to Dr. Metcalfe and since Bazile and Ann once shared the same throne in the 1948 Pilgrimage what could be more appropriate than for them to make *Fair Oaks* their home today as husband and wife?

Dining room and punkah at FAIR OAKS.

Three different woods—pine, cypress, and fruitwood—went into making of FAIR OAKS' Plantation Desk.

Flag of the 4th Louisiana Batallion.

SARAGOSSA

Between 1769 and 1787

Hidden away in the out-country, along the Old Nashville-New Orleans Post Road, is *Saragossa*. Of its actual building date written records are as vaguely silent as the mossy shadows that spill across this hidden world of Spanish daggers and lonely live oaks. Some hold that *Saragossa* had its beginnings as an early Spanish fortress. Others say David Williams built *Saragossa* as a home, and that his young widow married Gov. Winthrop Sargent here in 1798.

But fortress or fireside, *Saragossa* was to have a string of owners that sounds like a page out of "Who's Who" of ante-bellum Natchez: the Jonathan Thompsons of *The Grove* and *Green Leaves*, Dr. Stephen Duncan of *Auburn*, the St. John Elliotts of *D'Evereux*, the Austin Williams family of *Ashburn* and finally the Walton Pembroke Smiths of *Kinmore* and *Ashland*.

It was Walton Smith, a direct descendant of the only niece of President Madison, who tore away the original third floor of *Saragossa* and lifted the second-story ceilings. About the same time Mr. Smith converted his father-in-law's "Stock Farm" into a 3000 acre plantation, to which Mrs. Smith attached the present name, *Saragossa*.

Life for a time, for the Smiths of *Saragossa*, was abundant enough. Then came the Civil War and young Austin W. Smith marched off to fight as an Ensign with the 4th Louisiana Battalion. Hanging above the living room mantel in *Saragossa* today is the flag he carried through every major battle of the Confederate Army of Tennessee. Nearby is a Jewish Bible, the same one Walton Smith held in his lap that dark Reconstruction day when an assassin's bullet spent itself in the heavy folds of its pages and spared his life.

Though Walton Pembroke Smith and most of the 3000 acres he ruled have gone the way of the ages, the mystic beauty of his home has somehow escaped untouched.

Walton Smith's Bible.

THE BRIARS

Circa 1812

Perched high on a bluff that overlooks the Mississippi River and the Louisiana lowlands across the way is *The Briars*, girlhood home of Varina Howell, "The Rose of Mississippi," and the apple of Jefferson Davis' eye.

Just who built *The Briars* no one can be sure. It is said, though, that this old plantation house was a wedding present from Col. James Kempe to his daughter Louise when she married William Burr Howell, son of a New Jersey governor and a cousin of Aaron Burr. A naval veteran of the War of 1812, legend has it that Mr. Howell spent many pleasant hours on the edge of the nearby bluffs watching the comings and goings of the river packets 200 feet below.

On May 7, 1826 a girl child was born to William and Louise Howell. Christened Varina by her parents this same girl, less than 19 years later, would stand before the white Adam mantel in the front parlor of *The Briars* and say her marriage vows with wiry, proud Jefferson Davis, future President of the Confederate States of America. And so *The Briars*, the birthplace of Varina Howell, became the first stepping-stone toward her elevation one day as the first and only First Lady of her beloved Southland.

As a touch of irony, less than a score of years later a stray shell from a Federal gunboat would tear away one of the front gallery posts of the Confederate President's wedding place. The Walter Irvine family was living at *The Briars* during the War and legend tells of a lemon pie sale once put on for Union troopers by Miss Mary Irvine to help pay for a crepe shawl she had ordered from New Orleans.

Jefferson Davis and Varina Howell were married in THE BRIARS' front parlor.

Although Alexander Keene Richards did not remarry until nine years after the death of his first wife, he was destined to receive a most unusual wedding present from his former in-laws—a portrait of their deceased daughter, seated forlornly on a coffin, a wilted rose at her breast. Mr. Richards was a great grandfather of the present owner of the BRIARS, Mrs. Charles Kelley.

RICHMOND
1770-1832-Circa 1850

Few dare argue that *Richmond* has a special flavor all its own. This fine old place is a rare blend of three distinctly different epochs in Natchez' history. The center section, and oldest portion of the house, smacks of pioneer simplicity. The front, rearing tall against the slanting rays of the afternoon sun, boasts the white-columned elegance of the Greek Revival period. At the rear is found the last addition which seems to lean to the Georgian Colonial in its stark severity.

If *Richmond's* exterior makes it Natchez' only "three-in-one" house its interior is a virtual treasure chest of priceless heirlooms—from its slave-operated shower stall to its richly ornate silver service, from its "sobering-up tub" to an original Gilbert Stuart family portrait that once sold for fifty cents. Here, too, in the front parlor, is the piano that accompanied Jenny Lind during "The Swedish Nightingale's" Natchez concert of 1851.

Since Levin R. Marshall purchased *Richmond* in the early 1830's for the now unheard of sum of $7500, this unique old place has fittingly remained in the hands of his descendants. One of these, the late Theodora Britton Marshall, was a co-author of "They Found It In Natchez," a well-known history of the Old Trace Country.

Richmond's double baby bed for twins is a real antique oddity.

This original Gilbert Stuart portrait was returned to RICHMOND some years ago by a young girl on horseback. It was a gift to Miss Audley Marshall from a cousin who, for fifty cents, had retrieved the painting from "Aunt Kitty" Harris, a former Marshall slave.

The likes of RICHMOND'S hand-pumped shower stall were once outlawed in the East as being unsanitary. It seems the body servants of that day were somewhat negligent about emptying the water from one bath to the next. The "sobering-up tub," however, suffered no such disfavor.

SPRINGFIELD
Circa 1790

Out of the lush, loamy bosom of *Springfield* plantation bloomed one of the most beautiful but tragic romances in American history. It was here in August of 1791 that Rachel Donelson Robards said her marriage vows with quick-tempered, hard-fisted Andrew Jackson of Tennessee. As Rachel and Andrew stood hand-in-hand that summer day before Magistrate Thomas Green, who could know that Rachel still belonged to another man—that her divorce from her first husband, the insanely jealous Lewis Robards had never been finalized by the Virginia Legislature?

Whether the delay was intentional on the part of Robards or due to some quirk in the law an undeserved stigma would hover in the wings of Rachel and Andrew's lives forever.

Jackson had first known the hospitality of *Springfield* plantation some two years before, when he had followed the Trace south from Nashville and set up a trading post at the mouth of nearby Bayou Pierre. Then, a young man of 22 on his way up in the world, the lean and ambitious Jackson had sought to meet the needs of the surrounding gentry with everything from rare French wines to dark-skinned plantation hands. It was these business enterprises along the Bayou that one day took him back to Nashville and his first meeting with Rachel Robards, the soft-eyed daughter of the Widow Donelson and the one single love of his long, colorful life.

Coincidence would have it that Jackson's friends, the Greens of *Springfield,* were relatives of the Donelsons of Nashville and he must have been overjoyed that day when the Widow, fearful for her daughter's well-being at the hand of the jealous Robards, asked Andrew to see Rachel down the Trace to the safety of her kinsmen near Natchez.

Like Jackson before her, Rachel Robards was quick to gain a wide circle of friends in the Old Trace Country and here, for the 15 months that preceded their marriage, she and Andrew knew some of their happiest days.

BRANDON HALL

Circa 1856

Hovering like a great, white giant on a hillock overlooking the Old Natchez Trace *Brandon Hall* has, in days gone by, seen more than its share of the glories and sorrows of life.

The first Gerard Brandon ventured into the Natchez country from Ireland in the 1750's, rolled up his sleeves and turned the sweat of his determined Irish brow into a 28,000 acre land empire. His son, also surnamed Gerard, with a flair for success of his own so added to his father's estate that he became "the largest indigo and cotton planter in the South" as well as the first native-born Governor of Mississippi.

By the time Gerard III took the family reins and began about 1856 to build *Brandon Hall* for his wife, Charlotte, it is obvious that he, like so many of his contemporaries, had succumbed to the Greek Revival era of elegance. Around his new home Gerard Brandon swung more than 300 feet of spacious galleries, lifted by classic columns and laced here and there in delicate iron. Inside, behind the handsomely recessed main entrance, were parlor rugs from the Orient, services of English silver, mantels of the finest Italian marble and great pier mirrors from France.

Even in the midst of such abundance the footfall of tragedy often echoed through *Brandon Hall*. In a span of six short years Garard and Charlotte buried seven of their children within the long shadows of their home.

After the Civil War *Brandon Hall* may well have passed to the ages had not the L. A. Whites come from Greenville in 1947 to make many much needed repairs. From the Whites *Brandon Hall* recently passed to Dr. Harold C. Hawkins and Mr. H. Hal Garner, who plan a complete restoration of the old glories that was the real *Brandon Hall*.

JEFFERSON MILITARY COLLEGE
1802

Before *Jefferson Military College* recently closed its doors it was the oldest military school in the United States, including West Point.

Founded May 13, 1802, by act of the Territorial Legislature, the college was named for President Thomas Jefferson, a very close friend of Gov. W. C. C. Claiborne.

Within its ancient red brick walls and upon the surrounding 100 acre campus *Jefferson Military College* has seen the scroll of history unfold. Here, beneath the twin live oaks of its entrance, Aaron Burr's first conspiracy hearing was held in 1807. Eight years afterwards, under these same oaks, Andrew Jackson pitched camp with his victorious veterans of the Battle of New Orleans.

Near the Burr Oaks is a granite marker that commemorates the adoption of the constitution that led to Mississippi's statehood, December 10, 1817. The passage of eight more years found the great Lafayette in the reviewing stand as the *Jefferson* cadet corps swung past in salute. Here, too, the famous naturalist, John James Audubon, served on the faculty for a time as drawing instructor.

Among the most honored names on the rolls of *Jefferson Military College* is that of Jefferson Davis, who once swaggered across this historic campus as a ten-year-old cadet.

MOUNT LOCUST
Circa 1780

Mount Locust recalls that day when the Natchez Trace was the most important land route between Nashville and the Old Southwest.

Following the American Revolution, as traffic on the old Trace increased so did the demand for overnight rest stops where a man could tuck a warm meal in his belly and wash the dust of a day's journey from his throat with a pitcher of hot ale. To meet this growing need, pioneer cabins beside this wilderness way began to take on the look of roadside inns with names like She-boss, Buzzard Roost, Old Factor's, and French Camp.

During the days of the Trace's greatest popularity, more than fifty of these frontier rest stops were sprinkled along this pioneer road from Nashville to New Orleans. The advent of the Steamboat Age in 1820, however, made two-way travel on the river possible at last and the wayside inns began to vanish as they had arisen—slowly, surely, and one by one.

.. *Mount Locust*, the last of its colorful contemporaries, was restored by the National Park Service in 1956.